Thomas Hermann

learning languages
Sprachen lernen
apprendre les langues
aprender idiomas

Edition Offenes Buch

Preface

For European cultures to grow closer it would be desirable if everyone at least spoke two foreign European languages. While some might reject this idea of the European Commission, or consider it utopian, others would certainly be open to it. After all, most of us studied one or more foreign languages at school. So, the question would simply be how to renew our knowledge in the most rewarding way.

One effective method is to work with bilingual books. Even if one's knowledge of a foreign language is very basic, it is easy to gain access to a text in this language, if the translation into the mother tongue is right next to it.

The present book applies this principle. The multilingual presentation enables anyone who is fluent in English, German, French or Spanish from there on to become more familiar with one or more of the other languages.

The texts were selected by means of two criteria: they should come from various areas of life; and they had to be as succinct as possible because it is in this way that new words are most easily memorized.

Vorwort

Für das Zusammenwachsen unserer Kulturen ist zu wünschen, dass jeder von uns neben seiner Muttersprache zwei weitere europäische Sprachen spricht. Manche Leute werden diese Idee der Europäischen Kommission zurückweisen oder sie für utopisch halten. Andere dagegen werden dafür offen sein; schließlich haben sich die meisten von uns in der Schule mit zumindest einer fremden Sprache beschäftigt. Die Frage wäre dann nur, auf welche Weise sich die alten Kenntnisse am besten neu beleben lassen.

Eine effektive Methode besteht darin, mit zweisprachigen Büchern zu arbeiten. Auch wenn jemand nur über eine schmale Basis in einer anderen Sprache verfügt, wird ihm der Zugang zu einem Text in dieser Sprache nicht schwer fallen, wenn eine Übersetzung dieses Texts in die Sprache beigefügt ist, in der er selber zuhause ist.

Das vorliegende Buch greift dieses Prinzip auf. Die mehrsprachige Fassung der Texte ermöglicht es allen, die gut deutsch oder englisch, spanisch oder französisch sprechen, von dort ausgehend in der einen oder anderen der weniger vertrauten Sprachen weiterzukommen.

Was die Auswahl der Texte betrifft, waren zwei Kriterien entscheidend. Zum einen hatten sie aus verschiedenen Lebensbereichen zu kommen. Und zum anderen sollten sie so konzentriert wie möglich sein - weil sich neue Worte aus einem sinnvollen Zusammenhang heraus sicher am besten einprägen.

Préface

Pour que les cultures européennes puissent se rapprocher, il serait souhaitable que chaque citoyen parle au moins deux langues étrangères. Quelques-uns rejetteront cette idée de la Commission européenne ou la trouveront utopique; d'autres seront sûrement favorables à cette vision. Après tout, la majorité d'entre nous a appris une ou deux langues étrangères à l'école. Il ne s'agirait donc que de rafraîchir au mieux nos connaissances empoussiérées.

Une méthode efficace consiste à travailler avec des livres bilingues. Même pour celui qui ne possède que de rudimentaires connaissances d'une langue, il sera facile d'accéder à un texte s'il le trouve en même temps traduit dans une langue qu'il parle couramment.

Le présent livre applique ce principe. Grâce à la présentation multilingue des textes, celui qui parle couramment le français ou l'anglais, l'allemand ou l'espagnol, se sentira bientôt plus familier avec une ou plusieurs de ces langues.

Quant à la sélection des textes, elle a été faite selon deux critères : ils devaient provenir des domaines de la vie les plus variés. Et de plus, ils devaient être le plus succinct possible, car c'est dans un texte condensé qu'on mémorise le mieux les mots nouveaux.

Prefacio

Para que las culturas europeas se acercasen más, sería deseable que cada ciudadano hablase por lo menos dos idiomas extranjeros. Mientras que unos rechazarán esta noción de la Comisión Europea o la considerarán utópica, otros, seguramente, se abrirán a esta visión. Por fin, la mayoría de nosotros, en el colegio, hemos estudiado una o dos lenguas extranjeras. Así, la pregunta sería simplemente cómo refrescar el conocimiento anterior de una manera gratificante.

Un método eficaz consiste en trabajar con libros bilingües. Aunque alguien tenga solamente un conocimiento básico de una lengua extranjera, hallará con facilidad acceso a un texto en ésta si yuxtapone la traducción en un idioma en el que se mueva con soltura.

Este libro recoge este principio. Con la presentación multilingüe de los textos cortos, cada uno que hable con fluidez el inglés o el alemán, el español o el francés, estará, a partir de ahí, en condiciones de adquirir más familiaridad con otro u otros de estos idiomas.

Para la selección de los textos hubo dos criterios. Debían proceder de las áreas de vida más variadas. Y debían ser lo más sucintos posible, puesto que es en un texto condensado donde mejor se memorizan las nuevas palabras.

Light is refracted in the crystal; it sparkles.

La lumière se réfracte dans le cristal. Il scintille.

Das Licht bricht sich im Kristall. Er funkelt.

La luz se refracta en el cristal que brilla.

Reality is refracted within the language we speak.

our native language

The language we speak is the key to our way of thinking.

La réalité se réfracte dans la langue que nous parlons.

notre langue maternelle

La langue que nous parlons est la clé de notre mode de pensée.

Die Wirklichkeit bricht sich in der Sprache, die wir sprechen.

unsere Muttersprache

Die Sprache, die wir sprechen, ist der Schlüssel zu unserem Denken.

La realidad se refracta en el idioma que hablamos.

nuestra lengua materna

El idioma que hablamos es la llave a nuestro modo de pensar.

How is it possible that something exists?

Who created the universe? Who or what called the universe into existence?

Does God exist?

What is the cause of all causes?

origin

Comment est-il possible que quelque chose existe?

Qui a créé l'univers? Qui ou quoi a appelé l'univers à l'existence?

Dieu existe t-il?

Quelle est la cause des causes?

origine

Wie kann es sein, dass etwas existiert?

Wer hat das Universum geschaffen? Wer oder was hat das Universum hervorgebracht?

Existiert Gott?

Was ist die eigentliche Ursache?

Ursprung

¿Cómo es posible que algo exista?

¿Quién creó el universo? ¿Quién o qué llamó al universo a la existencia?

¿Existe Dios?

¿Cuál es la causa de las causas?

origen

The shortest form of world literature is the Haiku: a Japanese poem that consists of seventeen syllables in three lines.

This conciseness calls for the most careful use of words.

The challenge of a Haiku is, despite its rigorous form, to express an aspect of life with complete naturalness.

to renounce	renouncement
simplicity	
unadorned	
essence	essential

La forme la plus courte de la littérature mondiale est le poème japonais haïku. Il est composé de dix-sept syllabes en trois lignes.

Cette concision requiert un emploi très précis des mots.

Le défi du haïku consiste à exprimer un aspect de la vie d'une manière aussi naturelle que possible, tout en respectant sa forme rigoureuse.

renoncer	renoncement
simplicité	
sans fioritures	
essence	essential

Die kürzeste Form der Weltliteratur ist das Haiku: ein japanisches Gedicht, das aus siebzehn Silben in drei Zeilen besteht.

Diese Prägnanz verlangt eine äußerste Sorgfalt im Umgang mit den Worten.

Die Herausforderung des Haiku liegt darin, seiner strengen Form zum Trotz einen Aspekt des Lebens so natürlich wie möglich zum Ausdruck zu bringen.

verzichten   Verzicht

Einfachheit

ungekünstelt

Essenz   wesentlich

La forma más corta de la literatura mundial es el Haiku: un poema japonés que consiste de diecisiete sílabas en tres lineas.

Esta concisión requiere un empleo muy cuidadoso de las palabras.

El reto del Haiku es expresar un aspecto de vida, a pesar de la austeridad de su forma, con mayor naturalidad.

renunciar   renuncia

simplicidad

sin adornos

esencia   esencial

Towards evening Ryokan returns to his hut.
It is empty. A thief has been there.

As the full moon rises and shines through the small window, Ryokan smiles to himself. *What luck, the moon is still there ...*

Le soir, Ryokan revient à sa cabane.
Elle est vide. Un voleur est venu.

La pleine lune se lève et brille à travers la petite fenêtre. Ryokan sourit. *Quelle chance, la lune est toujours là ...*

Es wird Abend. Ryokan kommt zurück in seine Hütte.
Sie ist leer. Ein Dieb war da.

Der volle Mond geht auf und scheint durch das kleine Fenster. Ryokan lächelt.
Wie schön - der Mond ist noch da ...

Un día por la tarde Ryokán vuelve a su cabaña.
Está vacía. Estuvo un ladrón.

La luna llena sale y brilla por la pequeña ventana. Ryokán sonríe. *¡Qué bien!*
La luna todavía está ...

The greatest benefit of space exploration was not the technological progress, such as learning to launch rockets.

Its real benefit for humanity was to see earth, our home, from beyond: the pictures of the blue planet.

Le véritable bénéfice de l'exploration spatiale ne fut pas le progrès technique, le lancement de fusées par exemple.

Le bénéfice réel de la découverte spatiale pour l'humanité a été de voir la terre d'en haut : les images de la planète bleue.

Der eigentliche Gewinn für den Menschen durch seinen Aufbruch ins All war wohl nicht der technische Fortschritt, wie das Raketenschießenlernen.

Der bedeutendste Gewinn der Weltraumfahrt für die Menschheit lag darin, die Erde, unser Zuhause, aus einem Abstand zu sehen: die Bilder des blauen Planeten.

El beneficio más grande de la exploración del espacio no ha sido el progreso tecnológico, como aprender a lanzar cohetes.

Su beneficio real para la humanidad ha sido ver nuestro hogar desde afuera: las imágenes del planeta azul.

Life is just a loan.

We are simply guests in this world.

Life doesn't belong to us.

Most people only begin to appreciate life when they are on the point of losing it.

La vie nous a seulement été prêtée.

Nous ne sommes que des invités dans ce monde.

La vie ne nous appartient pas.

La plupart des gens commencent seulement à apprécier la vie quand ils sont sur le point de la perdre.

Das Leben ist uns nur geliehen.

Wir sind nur zu Gast in dieser Welt.

Das Leben gehört uns nicht.

Die meisten Menschen beginnen das Leben erst zu schätzen, wenn sie dabei sind es zu verlieren.

La vida no es más que un préstamo.

Somos simplemente huéspedes en este mundo.

La vida no nos pertenece.

La mayoría de los humanos solamente comienzan a apreciar la vida cuando están a punto de perderla.

It doesn't matter how many years there are in a life, but how much life there is in the years.

quality of life

intensity

a full life

what really matters

Peu importe combien d'années compte une vie, l'important, c'est combien de vie il y a dans ces années.

qualité de vie

intensité

une vie pleine

ce qui compte réellement

Es kommt nicht so sehr darauf an, wieviel Jahre ein Leben hat. Sondern darauf, wieviel Leben in den Jahren ist.

Lebensqualität

Intensität

ein erfülltes Leben

was wirklich zählt

No importa tanto cuántos años contiene una vida, sino cuánta vida hay en los años de un ser humano.

calidad de la vida

intensidad

una vida llena

lo que cuenta realmente

What separates man from life is that he tries to hold on to it.

That he cannot let go

to cling to

to grasp

attachment

Ce qui sépare l'homme de la vie, c'est qu'il tente de l'attrapper.

Qu'il ne peut pas lâcher prise.

se cramponner à

saisir

fixation

Was den Menschen vom Leben trennt, ist, dass er es festhalten will.

Dass er nicht loslassen kann.

sich klammern an

greifen

Verhaftung

Lo que separa al hombre de la vida es que intenta agarrarla.

Que no sabe soltar.

aferrarse a

agarrar

apego

Our ego considers itself the centre of the world.

It tries to create its own eternity.

transitory

futility

rebellion against reality

to insist
to take oneself seriously

plumage
vanity

Notre égo se prend pour le centre du monde.

Il essaie de créer sa propre éternité.

transitoir

futilité

rébellion contre la réalité

insister
se prendre au sérieux

plumage
vanité

Unser Ego hält sich für das Zentrum der Welt.

Es versucht seine eigene Ewigkeit zu schaffen.

vorübergehend

Vergeblichkeit

Aufstand gegen die Wirklichkeit

insistieren
sich selbst wichtig nehmen

Gefieder
Eitelkeit

Nuestro ego se considera el centro del mundo.

Intenta crear su propia eternidad.

transitorio

futilidad

rebeldía contra la realidad

insistir
tomarse en serio

plumaje
vanidad

Man lives in a prison as long as his thoughts and feelings aren't directed towards the whole, Einstein says, and his task is to expand his consciousness to include everything and to extend his compassion to all beings.

Evolution has an aim: Consciousness is its goal.

In man the universe becomes aware of itself, the philosophers tell us.
    A poet might say: It opens its eyes through us.

L'homme est enfermé dans une prison tant que ses pensées et ses sentiments ne sont pas dirigés vers le grand Tout, dit Einstein. Et son rôle est d'élargir sa conscience pour inclure l'ensemble et d'étendre sa compassion à tous les êtres.

L'évolution a un but : la conscience est son objectif.

Avec l'être humain, l'univers devient conscient de lui même, nous disent les philosophes.
    Comme dirait un poète : il ouvre les yeux au travers de nous.

Der Mensch befindet sich in einem Gefängnis, sagt Einstein, solange sich sein Denken und Fühlen nicht auf das Ganze richtet. Und die Aufgabe besteht darin, das Bewusstsein zu erweitern, bis es am Ende alles umfasst, und darin, das Mitgefühl auf alles Lebendige auszudehnen.

Die Evolution hat ein Ziel. Das Ziel ist Bewusstsein.

Im Menschen wird sich das Universum seiner selbst bewusst, sagen die Philosophen.
Wie ein Dichter sagen könnte: Es schlägt die Augen in uns auf.

El hombre se encuentra en una prisión mientras sus pensamientos y sentimientos no se dirijan hacia el todo, dice Einstein. Y su tarea es extender su conciencia hacia todo Ser y expandir su compasión a todo lo vivo.

La evolución tiene una meta: la conciencia es su objetivo.

Con el ser humano el universo se hace conciente de si mismo, los filósofos nos dicen.
Un poeta diría: abre sus ojos a través de nosotros.

Thomas More, on the day of his decapitation: *We are all in the same cart, on our way to death; so how can one hate or wish anybody harm?*

I have never met anyone who, on his deathbed, repented having done too much good. (Don Bosco)

Thomas Morus, le jour de sa décapitation : *Nous sommes tous dans cette charrette, en route vers la mort; ainsi, comment peut-on haïr ou souhaiter du mal à quelqu'un?*

Je n'ai jamais rencontré personne qui, sur son lit de mort, ait déploré avoir fait trop de bien. (Don Bosco)

Thomas Morus vor seiner Hinrichtung: *Sind wir auf unserem Weg zum Tod nicht alle im selben Wagen? Wie kann dann jemand hassen oder einem anderen Unheil wünschen?*

Noch nie habe ich jemanden getroffen, der sich auf dem Totenbett darüber beklagt hätte, zuviel Gutes getan zu haben. (Don Bosco)

Tomás Moro, el día que fue decapitado: *Estamos todos en el mismo carro, camino de la muerte; así ¿cómo puede uno odiar o desearle mal a nadie?*

Jamás he encontrado a nadie que en el lecho de muerte deplorase haber hecho demasiado bien. (Don Bosco)

Death is the best adviser.

to distinguish the important from the unimportant

distance

detachment

La mort est le meilleur conseiller.

distinguer l'important de ce qui n'est pas important

distance

détachement

Der Tod ist der beste Ratgeber.

das Wichtige vom Unwichtigen unterscheiden

Abstand

Gelassenheit

La muerte es el mejor consejero.

distinguir entre lo importante y lo no importante

distancia

desapego

The Romans used waterclocks. Seneca writes: *A water clock is emptied not only by the last drop, but by each drop that fell before the last. In the same way, man dies every hour that he is alive and the last hour only brings to an end this dying.*

Life and death are like two closed trunks, both of which contain the key to the other.

Learning to live and learning to die are the same.

Les Romains utilisèrent des horloges à eau. Sénèque écrit : *Ce n'est pas seulement la dernière goutte qui vide l'horloge, mais aussi toutes les gouttes antérieures. De même, l'être humain meurt à chaque heure de sa vie, et ce processus de mort s'achève à la dernière heure.*

La vie et la mort sont comme deux coffres fermés, chacun contenant la clé de l'autre.

Apprendre à vivre, apprendre à mourir, c'est la même chose.

Die Römer hatten Wasseruhren. Seneca schreibt: *Eine Wasseruhr leert sich nicht nur mit dem letzten Tropfen, sondern mit jedem einzelnen. Genauso stirbt der Mensch mit jeder Stunde seines Lebens, und seine letzte bringt dieses Sterben nur zum Ende.*

Leben und Tod sind wie zwei verschlossene Truhen, deren jede den Schlüssel zu der anderen enthält.

Leben lernen und sterben lernen sind eins.

Los romanos usaron relojes de agua. Séneca escribe: *No es solamente la última gota la que vacía un reloj de agua sino también cada gota anterior. De la misma manera el hombre muere cada hora que vive, y la última solo cumple este proceso de morir.*

La vida y la muerte son como dos arcas cerradas, cada una de las cuales contiene la llave de la otra.

Aprender a vivir y aprender a morir es lo mismo.

The fear of death deprives us of the courage to live.

The only certainty in life is death.

Only the hour is uncertain.

The fear of death runs through our life like a fissure.

Fear of the inevitable makes us ill.

The samurai is not afraid of death. He meets it head on.

A samurai is always prepared for the end. This is the essence of his life.

La peur de la mort nous enlève le courage de vivre.

Dans la vie, la chose la plus sûre, c'est la mort.

La seule chose qui n'est pas sûre, c'est son heure.

La peur de mourir traverse notre vie comme une fêlure.

Craindre l'inéluctable nous rend malade.

Le samouraï ne craint pas la mort. Il va à sa rencontre la tête haute.

Le samouraï est toujours préparé à mourir. C'est le sel de sa vie.

Die Angst vor dem Tod nimmt uns den Mut zu leben.

Das einzig Sichere im Leben ist der Tod.

Ungewiss ist nur die Stunde.

Die Furcht vor dem Tod durchzieht unser Leben wie ein Riss.

Die Angst vor dem Unausweichlichen macht einen Menschen krank.

Der Samurai fürchtet den Tod nicht, sondern geht ihm mit erhobenen Haupt entgegen.

Ein Samurai ist auf seinen Tod immer vorbereitet; das macht sein Leben reich.

El miedo a la muerte nos quita el valor para vivir.

Lo único que es seguro en la vida es la muerte.

La única incertidumbre es la hora.

El miedo a morir atraviesa nuestra vida como un fisura.

Temer lo inevitable nos enferma.

El samurai no teme a la muerte. Va a su encuentro con la cabeza erguida.

El samurai siempre está preparado para morir. Esto es la sal de su vida.

We owe it to death that being born is not a punishment. (Seneca)

repetition

endless

C'est grâce à la mort qu'être né n'est pas une punition. (Sénèque)

répétition

sans fin

Wir verdanken es dem Tod, dass es keine Strafe ist, geboren zu sein. (Seneca)

Wiederholung

endlos

Es por la muerte que haber nacido no es un castigo. (Séneca)

repetición

infinito

Today is the first day of the rest of my life.

Many people feel inspired and encouraged by this saying.

But it also works the other way round.
   Live today as if it were the last day of your life.

Living this day as if it were the last does not mean sitting down to write the last farewells.
   It means to live the present day as the decisive one - as if it were the mirror of a whole life.

Aujourd'hui est le premier jour du reste de ma vie.

Pour beaucoup de gens, ce dicton est source d'inspiration et d'encouragement.

Mais l'inverse est vrai aussi.
   Considère le jour d'aujourd'hui comme le dernier de ta vie.

Vivre le jour présent comme si c'était le dernier, cela ne veut pas dire s'asseoir pour écrire une lettre d'adieu.
   Cela signifie vivre ce jour comme un jour décisif - comme si toute une vie s'y reflétait.

Heute ist der erste Tag vom Rest meines Lebens.

Viele Menschen fühlen sich inspiriert und ermutigt durch diesen Satz.

Aber er macht auch umgekehrt Sinn.
Lebe den heutigen Tag als ob es dein letzter sei.

Den gegebenen Tag wie seinen letzten zu betrachten heißt nicht, sich an den Tisch zu setzen und einen Abschiedsbrief zu schreiben.
Sondern diesen Tag als einen entscheidenden anzusehen, als ob er der Spiegel wäre eines ganzen Lebens.

Hoy es el primer dia del resto de mi vida.

Mucha gente se siente inspirada y animada por este dicho.

Pero también tiene sentido darle la vuelta.
Considera el día de hoy como el último de tu vida.

Vivir el día presente como si fuera el último no significa sentarse y escribir una carta de despedida.
Lo que significa es vivirlo como el decisivo. Como si fuera el espejo de toda una vida.

Most people postpone their life.

They hope that it will be better one day.

If only I were grown-up ...
If only I had job security ...
If only the kids were settled ...
If only I were retired ...

castles in the sky

La majorité des gens remettent leur vie à plus tard.

Ils espèrent qu'un jour, ça ira mieux.

Le jour où je serai grand ...
Le jour où j'aurai un emploi sûr ...
Le jour où mes enfants seront indépendants ...
Le jour où je serai à la retraite …

châteaux en Espagne

Die meisten Menschen schieben ihr Leben auf.

Sie hoffen darauf, dass es eines Tages besser sein wird.

Wenn ich nur schon groß wär ...
Wenn nur der Job mal sicher wäre ...
Wenn nur die Kinder schon auf eigenen Füßen stünden ...
Wenn ich nur endlich in Rente wäre ...

Luftschlösser

La mayoría de la gente pospone su vida.

Esperan que vaya a ser mejor un día.

Una vez que sea adulto ...
Una vez que tenga un puesto de trabajo seguro ...
Una vez que los niños hayan creado su propio hogar ...
Una vez que esté jubilado ...

castillos en el aire

Young people can't even imagine how older people experience time.

Time flies.

illusions

Time slips through our fingers.

Les jeunes ne peuvent pas s'imaginer ce que les vieux ressentent vis-à-vis du temps.

Le temps s'envole.

illusions

Le temps s'ecoule entre nos doigts.

Die Jungen haben keine Ahnung, wie sich die Zeit für die Alten anfühlt.

Die Zeit verfliegt.

Illusionen

Die Zeit zerrinnt einem zwischen den Fingern.

Los jóvenes no pueden imaginarse cómo los mayores experimentan el tiempo.

El tiempo vuela.

ilusiones

El tiempo se escapa entre los dedos.

Life is as brief as a flash of lightning. (Buddha)

Human life is fleeting, like the shadow of a flying bird. (The Talmud)

Life races along like a galloping horse. (Chuang Tse)

However brief life may be – it offers us the opportunity to choose who we want to be.

La vie est rapide comme l'éclair. (Buddha)

La vie humaine est fugace comme l'ombre d'un oiseau en vol. (Talmud)

La vie court comme un cheval au galop. (Tchouang Tse).

Pour aussi courte que soit la vie, elle nous offre l'opportunité de choisir qui nous voulons être.

Kurz nur, wie ein Blitzstrahl, leuchtet das Leben auf. (Buddha)

Flüchtig ist das menschliche Leben, wie der Schatten eines fliegenden Vogels. (Aus dem Talmud)

Unser Leben ist wie ein vorbeigaloppierendes Pferd. (Tschuang Tse)

Wie kurz auch immer das Leben sein mag - es gibt uns die Gelegenheit zu wählen, wer wir sind.

La vida es corta como un relámpago. (Buda)

La vida humana es fugaz como la sombra de un pájaro volando. (El Talmud)

La vida pasa como un caballo galopante. (Tchuang Tse)

Por muy corta que sea la vida, nos ofrece la oportunidad de elegir quién queremos ser.

If someone were able to focus his thoughts towards one goal, he could achieve almost anything.

Discipline is the ability not to forget what one really wants.

Si quelqu'un était capable de diriger ses pensées vers *un* but, il pourrait réaliser presque tout.

La discipline est la capacité de ne pas oublier ce que l'on veut vraiment.

Wäre jemand fähig, seine Gedanken unbedingt auf ein Ziel zu richten, er könnte beinahe alles erreichen.

Disziplin ist die Fähigkeit, nicht zu vergessen, was man wirklich will.

Si alguien fuera capaz de dirigir sus pensamientos hacia *una* meta, podría conseguir casi todo.

La disciplina es la capacidad de no olvidar lo que uno quiere realmente.

We think our thoughts are ours. But in fact they have a life of their own.

In meditation, the beginner experiences thoughts as incessantly jumping like fleas from right to left, backwards and forwards.

restlessness

silence

inner dialogue

Who is able to say what he will think tomorrow or even in two minutes?

Nous croyons que nos pensées nous appartiennent. En fait, elles font ce qu'elles veulent.

Dans la méditation, le débutant fait l'expérience que ses pensées sautent sans cesse, de gauche à droite, d'avant en arrière, comme les puces.

inquiétude

silence

dialogue interne

Qui est capable de prédire ce qu'il pensera demain ou même dans deux minutes?

Wir glauben, in unseren Gedanken frei zu sein. In Wahrheit drehen sie sich aber um sich selbst.

Wer zu meditieren beginnt, macht die Erfahrung, dass sich die Gedanken nicht befehlen lassen, sondern wie Flöhe sind, die unablässig durcheinanderspringen.

Unruhe

Schweigen

innerer Dialog

Wer ist in der Lage zu sagen, was er morgen oder auch nur in zwei Minuten denken wird?

Creemos que nuestros pensamientos son nuestros. Pero, de hecho, siguen su propio rumbo.

En la meditación, el principiante experimenta cómo sus pensamientos saltan como pulgas de un lado para otro sin parar.

inquietud

silencio

diálogo interno

¿Quién es capaz de predecir lo que pensará mañana o incluso dentro de dos minutos?

Meditation does not mean thinking.

Neither does meditation mean suppressing arising thoughts.

Don't fight against them, the Zen Master says. *Let them come. Let them go.*
Let them pass through the mind like the clouds drifting in the sky.

appear   disappear

Méditer ne signifie pas penser.

La méditation ne signifie pas non plus s'empêcher de penser.

Ne lutte pas contre tes pensées, dit le maitre Zen. *Laisse-les venir et permet leur de s'en aller.*
Laisse-les de défiler et observe-les, comme des nuages dans le ciel.

apparaître   disparaître

Meditieren heißt nicht, seinen Gedanken nachzuhängen.

Ebensowenig bedeutet es, aufkommende Gedanken zu unterdrücken.

Kämpfe nicht gegen sie an, sagt der Zen-Meister. *Lass sie kommen. Lass sie gehen.*

Lass sie vorbeiziehen, und beobachte sie, wie Wolken unter einem blauen Himmel.

erscheinen   verschwinden

Meditar no significa pensar.

Tampoco significa suprimir los pensamientos.

No luches contra ellos, el maestro Zen dice. *Déjalos venir y deja que se vayan.*

Permítelos pasar y obsérvalos, como a las nubes en el cielo.

aparecer   desaparecer

Our thoughts and emotions are like the waves of the ocean.

They are nothing but form.

They have no origin of their own.

So meditation is not about controlling our thoughts. It is about realizing that they are without essence.

Nos pensées et nos émotions sont comme les vagues de l'océan.

Ce ne sont que des formes.

Elles n'ont pas d'origine propre.

Ainsi, dans la méditation, il ne s'agit pas d'acquérir le contrôle de ses pensées. Il s'agit de réaliser qu'elles n'ont pas d'essence propre.

Unsere Gedanken und Gefühle sind wie die Wellen des Meers.

Sie sind nichts als Form.

Sie haben keinen eigenen Ursprung.

So geht es beim Meditieren nicht darum, seine Gedanken unter Kontrolle zu bekommen. Sondern zu begreifen, dass nichts Wirkliches in ihnen ist.

Nuestros pensamientos y emociones son como las olas del océano.

Solamente son forma.

Carecen de cualquier origen propio.

Así, en la meditación no se trata de adquirir control sobre los pensamientos. Se trata de llegar a comprender que no tienen esencia alguna.

Spiritual life does not necessarily make one withdraw from the world; rather it should inspire one to face the tasks and challenges of daily life.

Real enlightenment does not make someone close his eyes, but brings one to live the Here and Now in full awareness.

What would be the point of enlightenment if it prevented someone from playing with his children?

Une vie spirituelle ne mène pas nécessairement au retrait du monde, elle devrait plutôt inspirer pour affronter les tâches et les défis de la vie quotidienne.

La véritable illumination ne conduit pas à fermer les yeux. Elle fait vivre *ici et maintenant*, en pleine conscience.

Que serait le bénéfice de l'illumination si elle empêchait l'homme de jouer avec ses enfants?

Ein spirituelles Leben führt nicht notwendigerweise dazu, sich aus der Welt zurückzuziehen; eher sollte es dazu animieren, sich den Aufgaben und den Herausforderungen des täglichen Lebens zu stellen.

Der wirklich Erleuchtete wird seine Augen nicht verschließen. Sondern das Hier und Jetzt ganz bewusst leben.

Was wäre der Sinn des Erleuchtetseins, wenn es einen davon abhielte, mit seinen Kindern zu spielen?

Una vida espiritual no necesariamente le mueve a uno a retirarse del mundo; más bien debería inspirarle a enfrentarse a las tareas y los retos de la vida diaria.

La iluminación verdadera no lleva a una persona a cerrar sus ojos, sino a vivir el Aquí y el Ahora con plena conciencia.

¿Cual sería el beneficio de la iluminación si le impidiese a uno jugar con los niños?

If a seeker met God in his meditation and then was approached by his hungry neighbour, he would please God more by standing up and filling a bowl for him than by keeping on meditating, Master Eckhart said.

Si un chercheur dans sa méditation rencontrait Dieu et que son prochain affamé s'approchait de lui, Dieu préfèrerait qu'il se lève et remplisse un bol, plutôt qu'il reste plongé dans sa méditation, a dit Maitre Eckart.

Wenn ein Sucher beim Meditieren Gott begegnete, und dann käme ein hungriger Nachbar vorbei, gefiele es Gott mehr, wenn er aufstünde und dem Nachbarn eine Schale füllte, als wenn er weiter meditierte, sagte Meister Eckhart.

Si un buscador en su meditación encontrase a Dios y entonces se le acercara su vecino hambriento, a Dios le agradaría que se levantara y llenara un bol para él en vez de seguir meditando, dijo Maestro Eckhart.

Many so-called Third World countries barely manage to feed their people –
while in the rich countries large quantities of food are destroyed with the only
aim of stabilizing prices.

consumer society

abundance

satiation

malnutrition

scarcity

Nombre de pays du soit-disant tiers monde réussissent à peine à alimenter
leur population, alors que dans les pays riches, on détruit de grandes quantités
d'aliments a la seule fin de maintenir le niveau des prix.

société de consommation

abondance

satiété

sous-alimentation

carence

Viele Länder der sogenannten Dritten Welt sind kaum in der Lage, ihre Bevölkerung zu ernähren, während in den reichen Ländern Unmengen von Lebensmitteln vernichtet werden, nur um die Preise stabil zu halten.

Konsumgesellschaft

Überfluss

Übersättigung

Unterernährung

Mangel

Muchos países del así llamado tercer mundo apenas consiguen alimentar a su gente mientras que en los países ricos se desechan grandes cantidades de alimentos con el único objetivo de estabilizar los precios.

sociedad de consumo

abundancia

hastío

subalimentación

carencia

Why is there so much misery in the world?

What answer can be given to this simple question? Why has so little humane progress been achieved, despite all the technological means we have at our disposal nowadays?

The reason is that, until now, the economical structures have not been directed towards qualitative growth.

sustainability

pillage

poverty

Pourquoi y a t-il tant de misère dans le monde?

Quelle réponse peut-on donner à cette simple question? Pourquoi le progrès humain n'est-il pas plus avancé alors que nous disposons aujourd'hui de tant de moyens techniques ?

La raison est, que, jusqu'à maintenant, les structures économiques ne sont pas centrées sur la croissance qualitative.

sostenibilité

pillage

pauvreté

Warum ist so viel Elend in der Welt?

Welche Antwort gibt es auf diese einfache Frage? Weshalb ist es zu so wenig menschlichem Fortschritt gekommen, bei all den technischen Möglichkeiten, die wir heute haben?

Der Grund liegt darin, dass sich die Wirtschaftsstrukturen bis heute nicht an qualitativem Wachstum orientieren.

Nachhaltigkeit

Plünderung

Armut

¿Por qué hay tanta miseria en el mundo?

¿Qué respuesta se puede dar a esta pregunta simple? ¿Por qué no se ha conseguido más progreso humano con todos los medios tecnológicos de los que disponemos hoy día?

La razón es que las estructuras económicas, hasta ahora, no están enfocadas hacia un crecimiento cualitativo.

sostenibilidad

pillaje

pobreza

Following the definition of the Gross National Product general affluence grows if a tornado causes widespread devastation, due to its beneficial effect on employment.

According to this logic, our prosperity increases when containers are washed overboard or even better, when the whole ship capsizes - because this means that a replacement has to be delivered, which, in turn, stimulates production.

If one part of the population is employed in digging holes, while the other part is busy filling them in, our economists tend to call this a sound and thriving economy.

Selon la définition du produit intérieur brut, la prospérité d'un pays augmente chaque fois qu'une tornade occasionne des dévastations à grande échelle, car elle a des effets positifs sur l'emploi.

Dans cette même logique, notre richesse s'accroît lorsque des containers passent par dessus bord ou mieux encore si le bateau coule. Car cela veut dire que la marchandise doit être remplacée, ce qui finalement relance la production.

Quand la moitié de la population est occupée à creuser des trous et l'autre moitié passe son temps à les boucher, nos économistes ont tendance à appeler cela une économie florissante.

Der Definition des Bruttosozialprodukts entsprechend steigt der allgemeine Wohlstand, wenn ein Wirbelsturm zu weitflächigen Verwüstungen führt, der positiven Wirkung wegen, die der Wiederaufbau auf die Beschäftigung hat.

Nach dieser Logik fördert es unseren Wohlstand, wenn Container über Bord gehen, oder besser noch der ganze Frachter kentert, weil dann ja Ersatz zu schaffen ist - was sich günstig auf die Produktionszahlen auswirkt.

Wenn die eine Hälfte der Bevölkerung damit beschäftigt ist, Gräben auszuheben, und die andere damit, sie wieder zuzuschütten, dann neigt der Wirtschaftswissenschaftler dazu, von einer gesunden Volkswirtschaft zu sprechen.

Según la definición del Producto Interior Bruto, la prosperidad común aumenta si un tornado produce una devastación a gran escala, por su efecto positivo sobre el empleo.

Dentro de esta lógica, nuestra riqueza se incrementa cuando un barco pierde contenedores o mejor aún todo el barco se hunde, ya que esto significa que se requiere un sustituto, lo que, a su vez, propulsa la producción.

Si una parte de los habitantes es empleada en cavar agujeros y la otra está ocupada en rellenarlos otra vez, nuestros economistas tienden a considerar esto una economía sana e intacta.

After the Cold War an international project was sought that could promote global collaboration, trust and peace and dissolve the rivalry and hostility of the past.

The outcome was the International Space Station.

Perhaps it wasn't the best decision.

Maybe it would have made more sense to focus our mental energies and technological development on preserving the ecological balance of the planet.
    That indeed would have been a peace-keeping project.

Après la guerre froide, on a cherché un projet international apte à promouvoir la coopération, la confiance et la paix et pour en finir avec les rivalités et les hostilités du passé.

Le résultat fut la station spatiale internationale.

Ce ne fut peut-être pas la meilleure décision.

Il aurait probablement été plus raisonnable de centrer l'énergie mentale et le progrès technique sur la préservation de l'équilibre écologique de la planète.
    En effet, cette orientation aurait été une véritable contribution à la paix mondiale.

Nach dem kalten Krieg war man auf der Suche nach einem Projekt, das für Zusammenarbeit, Vertrauen und Frieden stehen sollte und mit Hilfe dessen sich die Rivalität und Feindschaft der Vergangenheit auflösen lassen würde.

Das Ergebnis war die internationale Raumstation.

Was vielleicht nicht die beste Entscheidung war.

Vermutlich hätte es mehr Sinn gemacht, die geistigen Energien und den technischen Fortschritt auf den Erhalt des ökologischen Gleichgewichts des Planeten zu konzentrieren.
Und damit tatsächlich einen Beitrag zum Frieden auf dieser Welt zu leisten.

Después de la guerra fría se buscó un proyecto internacional que fomentara la colaboración, confianza y paz y que disolviera la rivalidad y la hostilidad del pasado.

El resultado fue la estación espacial internacional.

Quizás no fuera la mejor decisión.

Probablemente habría sido más razonable enfocar las energías mentales y el desarrollo tecnológico hacia la preservación del equilibrio ecológico del planeta.
Porque eso, efectivamente, hubiese contribuido a la paz mundial.

The glaciers are melting.

polar ice

sea level

greenhouse effect

Les glaciers fondent.

glace polaire

niveau de la mer

effet de serre

Die Gletscher schmelzen.

Polareis

Meeresspiegel

Treibhauseffekt

Los glaciares se están derritiendo.

el hielo polar

el nivel del mar

efecto invernadero

What will future generations think about us?

What would past generations have thought about us?

the descendants

future

responsibility

heritage

Que penseront de nous les générations futures?

Qu'auraient pensé de nous les générations précédentes?

les descendants

avenir

responsabilité

héritage

Was werden die zukünftigen Generationen über unsere Zeit denken?

Was würden frühere Generationen über uns gedacht haben?

die Nachkommen

Zukunft

Verantwortung

Erbe

¿Qué pensarán las generaciones futuras de nosotros?

¿Qué habrían pensado las generaciones pasadas de nosotros?

los descendientes

futuro

responsabilidad

herencia

Nothing demands as much character as going against the tide and saying *No*,
Kurt Tucholsky thought.

He was mistaken.

There is something that demands even more character: to admit an error to
oneself and to others.

open-minded   narrow-minded

theory   hypothesis   premise

a fixed idea   dead end

prevailing opinion

Rien ne nécessite autant de caractère que d'aller à contre-courant et de dire *Non*,
pensait Kurt Tucholsky.

Il s'est trompé.

Il y a quelque chose qui requiert encore plus de caractère : admettre une erreur
envers soi-même et les autres.

a l'esprit ouvert   d'esprit étroit

théorie   hypothèse   prémisse

une idée fixe   cul-de-sac

opinion prédominante

Nichts verlangt so viel Charakter wie sich gegen den Strom der Zeit zu stellen und *Nein* zu sagen, war Tucholsky überzeugt.

Darin hat er sich getäuscht.

Es gibt etwas, was noch mehr Charakter verlangt: einen Irrtum vor sich selbst und vor anderen einzugestehen.

aufgeschlossen   engstirnig

Theorie   Hypothese   Prämisse

eine eingefahrene Idee   Sackgasse

herrschende Meinung

Nada requiere tanto carácter como ir a contracorriente y decir *No*, pensó Kurt Tucholsky.

Se equivocó.

Hay algo que requiere aún más carácter: admitir el error ante uno mismo y confesarlo frente a los demás.

abierto   estrecho de miras

teoría   hipótesis   premisa

una idea fija   callejón sin salida

opinión prevaleciente

For the defenders of communism it must have been hard to realize that their world-view was based on a fundamental error of thinking.

But neither do the supporters of capitalism have much of a reason to be pleased with the way certain things have developed.

While one system was not able to fulfil the needs of the people, the other one faces the constant problem of how to sell people what they do not need.

Pour les partisans du communisme, il a dû être très difficile d'admettre que leur vision du monde reposait sur une fausse supposition.

Mais les supporters du capitalisme, eux non plus, n'ont pas de réelles raisons d'être contents du cours des choses.

Tandis qu'un système s'est avéré incapable de satisfaire les besoins de la population, l'autre est confronté à un problème constant : comment vendre aux gens ce dont ils n'ont pas besoin.

Für die Anhänger des Kommunismus muss es hart gewesen sein, einzusehen, dass sich ihre Vorstellung von der Welt auf einem fundamentalen Denkfehler gegründet hatte.

Die Vertreter des Kapitalismus können mit dem Gang der Dinge allerdings auch nur bedingt zufrieden sein.

Während das eine System nicht in der Lage war, die Bedürfnisse der Menschen zu decken, plagt sich das andere mit dem dauernden Problem, den Leuten zu verkaufen, was sie nicht brauchen.

Para los defensores del comunismo tiene que haber sido duro comprobar que su visión del mundo estaba basada en un error fundamental de su planteamiento.

Pero tampoco los partidarios del capitalismo tienen demasiados motivos para estar contentos con el desenvolvimiento de ciertas cosas.

Mientras que un sistema no era capaz de cubrir las necesidades de la gente, el otro tiene que hacer frente al constante problema de cómo vender a la gente lo que no necesita.

It's only half the truth that people enjoy smoking.

The other half is that the tobacco industry is striving to make them smoke.

The arms industry is probably not too interested in a peaceful world.

Those who have invested money in oil wells or nuclear reactors will not feel too enthusiastic about the success of renewable energies.

Dire que les gens aiment fumer, ce n'est qu'une partie de la vérité.

En fait, l'industrie du tabac fait tout ce qu'elle peut pour les amener à fumer.

Un monde pacifique n'est sans doute pas dans l'intérêt de l'industrie d'armement.

Ceux qui ont investi dans des puits de pétrole ou des centrales nucléaires ne seront pas très heureux du succès des énergies renouvelables.

Es ist nur ein Teil der Wahrheit, dass die Leute eben gerne rauchen.

Der andere ist, dass die Tabakindustrie alles unternimmt, dass sie rauchen.

Vielleicht ist die Rüstungsindustrie am Frieden nicht allzusehr interessiert.

Wer Geld ins Ölbohren oder in Atomkraftwerke investiert hat, wird über den Erfolg der erneuerbaren Energien nicht unbedingt begeistert sein.

Es solo una parte de la verdad que a la gente le gusta fumar.

La otra es que la industria del tabaco se esfuerza en que fume.

Probablemente, la industria de las armas no tiene demasiado interés en un mundo pacífico.

Los que han invertido en pozos de petróleo o en centrales nucleares, no sentirán demasiado entusiasmo por el éxito de las energías renovables.

The food industry insists on their right to keep secret how our food is produced.

And what it contains.

                                                    That's the world in which we live.

transparency

refusal

                                                    chocolate made of pig's blood

L'industrie alimentaire insiste sur le droit de ne pas dire comment est fabriqué ce que nous mangeons.

Et ce qu'il y a dedans.

                                                    C'est le monde dans lequel nous vivons.

transparence

refus

                                                    chocolat à base de sang de porc

Die Nahrungsmittelindustrie besteht auf dem Recht, im Dunkeln zu halten, wie unsere Lebensmittel hergestellt werden.

Und was sie enthalten.

Das ist die Welt, in der wir leben.

Transparenz

Weigerung

Schokolade aus Schweineblut

La industria de la alimentación insiste en el derecho de mantener en secreto cómo se produce lo que comemos.

Y lo que contiene.

Ese es el mundo en el que vivimos.

transparencia

negación

chocolate hecho con sangre de cerdo

Where democracy is taken for granted, it is lost.

Democracy is not self-sustaining.

vigilance

constitution

erosion

undermine

Considérer la démocratie comme une chose acquise, c'est la perdre.

La démocratie ne peut pas se soutenir elle-même.

vigilance

constitution

érosion

miner

Wo eine Demokratie für sicher gehalten wird, ist sie verloren.

Demokratie hält sich nicht von selbst.

Wachsamkeit

Verfassung

Erosion

aushöhlen

Dar la democracia por sentado significa perderla.

La democracia no es autosostenible.

vigilancia

constitución

erosión

minar

Former generations could only have dreamt of the living conditions that most of us in the Western World take for the most normal thing.

leisure
bookshop   library   concert hall
bicycle   hang glider
emergency numbers   ambulance
glasses   nail scissors
water tap
refrigerator
central heating

Les générations précédentes n'ont pu que rêver des conditions de vie que la majorité d'entre nous en Occident considèrent aujourd'hui comme la chose la plus normale du monde.

temps libre
librairie   bibliothèque   salle de concert
bicyclette   planeur
appel d'urgences   ambulance
lunettes   ciseaux à ongles
robinet
réfrigérateur
chauffage central

Die Menschen früherer Generationen haben nur träumen können von den Lebens-
bedingungen, die die meisten von uns im Westen für selbstverständlich halten.

Freizeit
Buchhandlung   Bibliothek   Konzertsaal
Fahrrad   Segelflugzeug
Notruf   Krankenwagen
Brille   Nagelschere
Wasserhahn
Kühlschrank
Zentralheizung

Las generaciones de antaño meramente habrían podido soñar con las condiciones
de vida que la mayoría de nosotros en occidente hoy tomamos como la cosa más
normal.

tiempo libre
librería   biblioteca   sala de conciertos
bicicleta   planeador
llamada de emergencia   ambulancia
gafas   tijeras para las uñas
grifo de agua
frigorífico
calefacción central

None of the previous generations had to face the possibility that humanity would destroy itself.

weapons of mass destruction

nuclear weapons

genetic engineering

biological weapons

chemical weapons

Aucune des générations du passé n'a dû affronter la possibilité que l'humanité pourrait s'autodétruire.

armes de destruction massive

armes nucléaires

technologie génétique

armes biologiques

armes chimiques

Keine der früheren Generationen hatte wie wir der Möglichkeit ins Auge zu sehen, dass die Menschheit sich selbst zerstören kann.

Massenvernichtungswaffen

Atomwaffen

Gentechnik

biologische Waffen

chemische Waffen

Ninguna de las generaciones pasadas tuvo que enfrentarse a la posibilidad de que la humanidad se destruyera a sí misma.

armas de destrucción masiva

armas nucleares

tecnología genética

armas biológicas

armas químicas

World War IV would not have been an option, because after World War III nothing of civilization would have remained; from then on, war would be waged with bludgeons, as Einstein pointed out.

During the Cuba Crisis the world was very close to the abyss.

And in the 1980s, American travel agencies suggested that their prospective clients should visit the old cathedrals and castles while it was still possible to do so.

Go and see Europe while it still exists.

It was anything but foreseeable that the Cold War would end the way it did.

La quatrième guerre mondiale n'aurait pas représenté une option, car après la troisième, il ne serait plus rien resté de la civilisation; par la suite, on aurait fait la guerre en brandissant des massues, comme le signalait Einstein.

Durant la crise de Cuba, le monde était au bord de l'abîme.

Et durant les années quatre-vingt, les agences de voyage américaines suggéraient à leurs clients potentiels de visiter les cathédrales et vieux châteaux tant que c'était encore possible.

Allez voir l'Europe tant que l'Europe existe.

Rien ne permettait de prévoir que la guerre froide connaîtrait la fin qu'elle a connue.

Einen vierten Weltkrieg hätte es nicht geben können. Denn nach dem dritten würde von der Zivilisation nichts übriggeblieben sein; danach würde, wie Einstein formulierte, der Krieg wieder mit Keulen geführt werden.

Während der Kubakrise hat die Welt sehr nah am Abgrund gestanden.

Und in den Achtzigern schlugen amerikanische Reiseveranstalter ihren geneigten Kunden vor, die alten Kathedralen und Schlösser zu besuchen, solange es noch möglich war.

Sehen Sie sich Europa an, solange es Europa gibt.

Es war alles andere als vorhersehbar, dass der Kalte Krieg so enden würde, wie er geendet *hat*.

Una cuarta guerra mundial no habría sido una opción. Porque después de la tercera no habría quedado nada de la civilización; después la guerra se continuaría con porras, como Einstein señaló.

Durante la crisis de Cuba el mundo estuvo muy cerca del abismo.

Y en los años ochenta, las agencias de viajes americanas sugirieron a sus clientes interesados visitar las catedrales y castillos antiguos mientras todavía fuera posible.

Vaya a ver Europa, mientras Europa aún exista.

No era nada predecible que la guerra fría terminara como lo hizo.

The explanation that the Warsaw Pact simply dissolved because it was beaten in the arms race is quite misleading. (Actually, it might be a rather dangerous one.)

If small North Korea - nuclear armed - can't be overcome, then how could this have been achieved with a dictatorial superpower?

The cause of the end of the Cold War was, that someone was bold enough to tear down the totalitarian structures in his country, stop the arms race, and thus cut through the vicious circle of fear between East and West.

As James Baker, the former Secretary of State of the United States, says: History will surely treat Gorbatschow very well.

L'idée que le pacte de Varsovie s'est dissout simplement parce qu'il a perdu la course aux armements ne va pas dans la bonne direction. (En effet, cela pourrait être une idée plutôt dangereuse.)

Si la petite Corée du Nord, avec si peu d'armes nucleaires, n'a pas pu être mise hors jeu, comment cela aurait-il été possible avec une super-puissance dictatoriale?

La cause de la fin de la guerre froide était qu'un homme fut assez courageux pour rompre avec les structures totalitaristes de son pays, arrêter la course aux armes et anéantir le cercle vicieux de la peur entre l'Est et l'Ouest.

Comme le dit James Baker, ancien secrétaire d'Etat des Etats Unis : L'histoire traiterait certainement Gorbatchev de manière très positive. :

Die Vorstellung, dass sich der Ostblock einfach deswegen aufgelöst hat, weil er nicht in der Lage war, im Rüstungswettlauf mitzuhalten, geht fehl. (In der Tat sollte sie als eine eher gefährliche Idee begriffen werden.)

Wenn das kleine, nuklear bewaffnete Nordkorea nicht totgerüstet werden kann - wie wäre das mit einer diktatorisch geführten Supermacht möglich gewesen?

Der Grund für das Ende des Kalten Krieges war, dass jemand den Mut hatte, sich den totalitären Strukturen in seinem Land entgegenzustellen, das Wettrüsten zu beenden und damit den Teufelskreis der Angst zwischen Ost und West zu durchbrechen.

Die Geschichte wird Gorbatschow sicherlich sehr gut behandeln. (James Baker, ehemaliger US-Außenminister)

La explicación que el Pacto de Varsovia se haya disuelto solamente por haber sido derrotado en la carrera armamentísta, resulta mas bien engañosa (De hecho puede llegar a ser bastante peligrosa.)

Como no era posible llevarle la delantera a la pequeña Corea del Norte con sus pocas armas nucleares ¿cómo habría sido posible conseguirlo con una superpotencia dictatorial?

La razón del fin de la guerra fría es que alguien tuvo el suficiente valor para romper con las estructuras totalitarias de su país, acabar con la carrera de armas y así romper el círculo vicioso del miedo entre Este y Oeste.

La Historia seguramente tratará a Gorbatchov muy bien. (James Baker, anterior ministro de Asuntos Exteriores de los Estados Unidos)

The question of whether cooperation or competition should be considered as the underlying principle of life has to become the key question in the dialogue between cultures.

with each other

against each other

La coopération ou la compétition, qu'est-ce qui doit être considéré comme le principe de base de la vie? C'est ce qui doit devenir la question cruciale dans le dialogue entre les cultures.

l'un avec l'autre

l'un contre l'autre

Die Frage, ob die Zusammenarbeit oder ob der Wettbewerb als das eigentliche Prinzip des Lebens gedacht werden soll, muss sich zur Kernfrage im Dialog der Kulturen entwickeln.

miteinander

gegeneinander

La cuestión de si es la cooperación o si es la competición que debe ser considerado como el principio básico de la vida tiene que hacerse la cuestión crucial en el diálogo entre las culturas.

uno con el otro

uno contra el otro

In the nineteenth century the idea was born that life is essentially a struggle for survival, and that became the dominant view.

In this perspective, the nature of life is described as a process of competition and selection rather than as coexisting life forms, which are interdependent and mutually supporting.

This vision left tragic results in its wake.

Au cours du dix-neuvième siècle, la notion s'imposait que la vie est essentiellement une lutte pour la survie.

Dans cette conception du monde, la vie est décrite comme un processus de compétition et de sélection, plutôt que comme une coexistence de formes de vie interdépendantes qui se soutiennent mutuellement.

Une vision qui aboutit à des conséquences tragiques.

Im Lauf des neunzehnten Jahrhunderts setzte sich die Idee durch, dass das Leben als ein immerwährender Überlebenskampf zu sehen ist.

Demnach ist das Leben ein Prozess des Wettbewerbs und der Auslese. Und nicht ein Miteinander von Lebensformen, die sich gegenseitig unterstützen und voneinander abhängig sind.

Es war eine Idee, die tragische Folgen hatte.

En el curso del siglo diecinueve fue imponiéndose la noción de que la vida, esencialmente, es una lucha por la supervivencia.

En esta concepción del mundo, la naturaleza de la vida se describe como un proceso de competición y de selección, más bién que como una coexistencia de formas de vida que son interdependientes y que se apoyan mutuamente.

Esta visión tuvo consecuencias trágicas.

How could a barbaric regime like National Socialism arise, that defined war as a law of human nature and declared as a birthright the erradication of other peoples?

The real reason for the concentration camps and World War II was not the humiliation after having lost World War I, neither was it the despair of the unemployed, as still written in quite some German schoolbooks.

The deeper reason was the conviction of being destined for world supremacy which was widespread in many nations.

Comment fut-il possible qu'apparaisse une idéologie barbare comme le national-socialisme, qui définit la guerre comme une loi de la nature humaine et déclara l'extermination d'autres peuples comme un droit de naissance?

Les camps de concentration et la seconde guerre mondiale ne sont pas dus à l'humiliation d'avoir perdu la première; ni non plus au désespoir de millions de chômeurs, comme l'enseignent toujours presque tous les manuels scolaires allemands.

La cause profonde résidait dans la notion très répandue dans de nombreuses nations que justement elles étaient investies du droit de suprématie mondiale.

Wie konnte es zu einer Ideologie wie dem Nationalsozialismus kommen? Einer Ideologie, die den Krieg als ein grundlegendes Gesetz des menschlichen Daseins definierte. Und die Auslöschung anderer Völker als ein Geburtsrecht des eigenen Volkes.

Der eigentliche Grund dafür, dass es zu den Konzentrationslagern und zum Zweiten Weltkrieg gekommen ist, war nicht die Demütigung, den ersten verloren zu haben, und es war auch nicht die Verzweiflung der Arbeitslosen - wie es bis heute noch fast durchgehend in den deutschen Schulbüchern steht.

Der tieferliegende Grund war die Überzeugung vieler Nationen, dass gerade sie es seien, denen es vom Schicksal vorherbestimmt sei, die Weltherrschaft anzutreten.

¿Cómo fue posible que un régimen bárbaro como el nacionalsocialismo surgiera? Régimen que definió la guerra como una ley de la naturaleza humana y declaró como un derecho de nacimiento la erradicación de otros pueblos.

La causa verdadera de los campos de concentración y de la II guerra mundial no fue la humillación de haber perdido la primera, ni tampoco la desesperación de los desempleados, como figura todavía en no pocos libros de texto alemanes.

La causa más profunda era la noción, muy extendida en muchas naciones, de que precisamente ellas estaban predestinadas a la supremacía mundial.

When school-children return from a visit to a former concentration camp like Auschwitz, they know they have been in touch with an unspeakable tragedy.

It is clear to them that something like this must never be repeated.

But how likely is it, that it never will be repeated?

What will happen if climate change deprives us of the living conditions basic to the survival of seven, eight or nine billion human beings? If spreading drought and floods bring about food shortages?

Quand des groupes scolaires reviennent de la visite d'un ancien camp de concentration comme Auschwitz, ils savent qu'ils ont été en contact avec une indicible tragédie.

Ils ont compris qu'une telle chose ne doit plus jamais se répéter.

Mais quelle est la probabilité que cela ne se répète pas?

Que se passera t-il si le changement climatique nous prive des conditions de vie nécessaires à la survie de sept, huit, ou neuf milliards d'êtres humains? Si la sécheresse et les inondations en augmentation aboutissent à des pénuries alimentaires?

Wenn Schulklassen aus einem ehemaligen Konzentrationslager wie Auschwitz zurückkommen, ist ihnen bewusst, dass sie mit einer unsagbaren Tragödie in Berührung gekommen sind.

Es steht ihnen vor Augen, dass sich Derartiges niemals wiederholen darf.

Aber wie wahrscheinlich ist es, dass es sich nicht wiederholt?

Was wird passieren, wenn uns der Klimawandel der notwendigen Lebensgrundlagen für sieben, acht oder neun Milliarden Menschen beraubt? Wenn zunehmende Dürren und Überflutungen die Nahrung knapp werden lassen?

Cuando los alumnos de un colegio regresan de una visita a un campo de concentración como Auswich, saben que han estado en contacto con una tragedia indecible.

Les queda claro que tal cosa nunca más se debe repetir.

Sin embargo ¿qué probabilidad hay de que una cosa así no se repita?

¿Qué pasará si el cambio climático nos priva de la base de vida necesaria para la supervivencia de siete, ocho o nueve mil millones de seres humanos? ¿Qué pasara si el incremento de sequías e inundaciones ocasiona estrecheces alimentarias?

Quite some people are convinced it's better not to face certain threatening developments.

They are afraid that imagining such scenarios could turn out to be self-fulfilling prophecies.

It is true that negative expectations can reinforce or even provoke the feared.

On the other hand, shutting one's eyes to a problem will not solve it: Only a problem which is recognized can be tackled.

The most dangerous fear is the fear of fear.

Beaucoup de gens sont convaincus qu'il vaut mieux ne pas ouvrir les yeux sur certains dévoloppements alarmants qui pourraient devenir réalité.

Ils craignent que le fait d'imaginer de tels scénarios ne fasse se réaliser ce dont ils ont si peur.

Il est vrai que les perspectives négatives peuvent renforcer ou même déclencher ce que l'on craint le plus.

D'autre part, ignorer un problème ne le résoudra pas : seul un problème reconnu comme tel peut être abordé.

Le plus dangereux, c'est la peur de la peur.

Viele Leute sind überzeugt davon, dass man sich gewisse drohende Entwicklungen besser nicht vor Augen führen sollte.

Sie befürchten, dass sich derartige Szenarien zu sich selbst erfüllenden Prophezeiungen entwickeln könnten.

Es ist wahr, dass eine negative Erwartungshaltung ein befürchtetes Geschehen verstärken oder es gar hervorrufen kann.

Auf der anderen Seite lässt sich ein reales Probleme nicht dadurch lösen, dass man die Augen vor ihm verschließt: Nur das Problem, das wahrgenommen wird, kann angegangen werden.

Die gefährlichste Angst ist die Angst vor der Angst.

Mucha gente está convencida de que sea mejor que ciertos desarrollos amenazadores no se consideren seriamente.

Temen que imaginarse tales escenarios, precisamente, pueda producir la realidad temida.

Cierto es que expectativas negativas pueden reforzar, o hasta producir, el resultado del que se tenía miedo.

Por otra parte, cerrar los ojos ante un problema no lo solucionará; solamente un problema que es reconocido como tal puede ser abordado.

El miedo al miedo es lo más peligroso.

Many people assume that they cannot change the world.

Actually, they *do* change it. If they do not influence it by their vote, they affect it by their silence.

We are not just witnesses, but also participants of history.

to think globally
to act locally

enemies of mankind
indifference
cowardice
indolence
resignation

                                                                    cynicism

De nombreuses personnes croient qu'elles ne peuvent pas changer le monde.

Mais en vérité, elles le changent en tout cas. Si elles ne l'influencent pas par leur voix, elles l'affectent par leur silence.

Nous ne sommes pas seulement témoins de l'histoire, nous en sommes aussi les acteurs.

penser globalement
agir localement

ennemis de l'humanité
indifférence
lâcheté
indolence
résignation

                                                                    cynisme

Viele Menschen glauben, sie könnten die Welt nicht verändern.

Sie verändern sie aber in jedem Fall. Wenn nicht durch ihre Stimme, dann durch ihr Schweigen.

Wir sind nicht nur Zeugen der Geschichte. Wir sind auch die, die sie schreiben.

global denken
vor Ort handeln

Feinde der Menschheit
Gleichgültigkeit
Feigheit
Trägheit
Resignation

Zynismus

Mucha gente cree que no puede cambiar el mundo.

La verdad es que sí que lo cambian; si no lo influencian a través de su voz lo afectan a través de su silencio.

No somos solamente testigos sino también partícipantes de la historia.

pensar globalmente
actuar localmente

enemigos de la humanidad
indiferencia
cobardía
pereza
resignación

cinismo

We get annoyed when we are stuck in a traffic jam.

What we don't think about is that we *are* the traffic jam.

blind spot

to be part of the problem or to be part of the solution

Nous sommes contrariés quand nous sommes bloqués dans un embouteillage.

Ce que nous ne prenons pas en compte, c'est que nous *sommes* l'embouteillage.

tache aveugle

faire partie du problème ou faire partie de la solution

Es regt uns auf, wenn wir im Stau stehen.

Woran wir nicht denken, ist, dass wir der Stau *sind*.

blinder Fleck

Teil des Problems oder Teil der Lösung sein

Nos fastidia cuando nos quedamos atrapados en un atasco.

Lo que no tenemos en cuenta es que *somos* el atasco.

punto ciego

formar parte del problema o formar parte de la solución

For a change to happen, a critical mass of consciousness is required.

It cannot be predicted when a certain change will occur. So any individual may cast the decisive vote.

But in fact *every* vote is a decisive one - because it is not only the last grain that tips the scales.

Avant que se produise un changement, il est nécessaire que s'accumule une masse critique de conscience.

On ne peut pas prévoir le moment où se fera le changement. Ainsi, la contribution de chaque individu de l'homme peut être le vote décisif.

En effet il n'y a pas que le dernier grain qui fait pencher la balance, mais chaque grain ajouté au précédent est décisif.

Ehe es zu einer Veränderung kommt, muss es eine kritische Masse des Bewusstseins geben.

Es ist unvorhersehbar, wann es zu einer bestimmten Veränderung kommt. Und damit kann jede Stimme die ausschlaggebende sein.

Aber in jedem Fall ist es nicht nur das letzte Korn, das einen Umschlag bewirkt. Nicht nur das letzte hat Gewicht. Sondern es ist jedes einzelne, das entscheidet.

Para que pueda ocurrir un cambio tiene que acumularse una masa crítica de conciencia.

No es predecible cuándo ocurrirá el cambio. Por eso la contribución de cualquier individuo puede ser el voto preponderante.

En efecto no es solamente el último grano el que hace inclinar la balanza. Es cada grano que ha sido añadido antes el que resulta ser el decisivo.

The editor wishes to express his gratitude to everyone who has contributed, in one way or another, to this book. Without them it wouldn't have come to be.
Special thanks for their helpfulness to:

Der Herausgeber bedankt sich bei allen, die zu diesem Buch in der einen oder der anderen Weise etwas beigetragen haben. Ohne sie wäre es nicht entstanden.
Besonderer Dank für ihre Hilfsbereitschaft richtet sich an:

L'éditeur exprime sa gratitude envers chaque personne ayant contribué d'une maniere ou d'une autre à ce livre. Sans eux, cela n'aurait pas été possible.
Remerciements spéciaux pour leur appui à :

El editor agradece a todos los que han contribuido - de una manera o otra - en este libro.Sin ellos no se habría hecho realidad.
Un agredecimiento especial por su ayuda se dirige a:

Roger Gonçalvez da Silva   Paola Tobalina Cuerda   Mike & Lilly Conway

Josefa Cristina Castillo   Gerda Schuil   Jörg Friedrich

We hope to be able to present a sequel to this book within the *Edition Offenes Buch (Edition Open Book)* by the end of 2011.

Therefore anyone who feels called to do so is invited to suggest if possible clear, powerful reflections from any area of life in English or in any of the other languages.

Bis Ende 2011 ist eine Fortsetzung dieses Bandes in der *Edition Offenes Buch* geplant.

Wir laden dazu ein, dafür eingängige, kraftvolle Gedanken - aus welchen Lebensbereichen auch immer vorzuschlagen - auf deutsch oder in einer der anderen drei Sprachen.

Nous espérons pouvoir présenter une suite à ce livre dans *l'Edition Offenes Buch (Edition Livre Ouvert)* avant la fin 2011.

A cet effet, nous invitons ceux qui se sentent inspirés à nous soumettre des propositions enrichissantes (d'un quelconque domaine de la vie) en français ou dans une des autres langues.

Esperamos poder presentar una continuación de este libro de la *Edition Offenes Buch (Edition Libro Abierto)* para finales de 2011.

Asi invitamos a todos los que se sientan inspirados para ello, sugerir reflexiones. Pueden derivar del ambito de vida que sea y figurar en espagnol o en una de las otras tres lenguas.

edition-offenes-buch@web.de

ibliografische Information der Deutschen Nationalbibliothek
ieDeutscheNationalbibliothekverzeichnetdiesePublikationinderDeutschenNationalbibliografie;
taillierte bibliografische Daten sind im Internet über http://dnb.d-nb.de abrufbar.

2011 Thomas Hermann

rstellung und Verlag: Books on Demand GmbH, Norderstedt

3N 9783842350946